Concertino
in G major.

O. Rieding Op. 24.

B. & Cº 6133
Made in England

Tous droits d'exécution réservés.

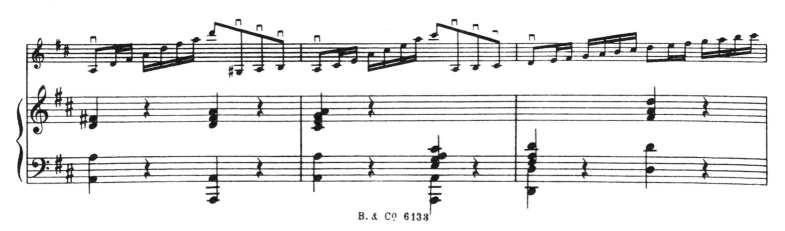

B. & Cº 6133

B. & Cº 6133

B. & Cᵒ 6133. 6773.13337.10269

Easy Concertos and Concertinos
for Violin and Piano

O. Rieding

Concertino
in G

Op.24
(1st, 3rd and 5th position)

Bosworth

Concertino
in G major.

Violino.

O. Rieding Op. 24.

Allegro moderato.

Copyright MCMIV by Bosworth & Co.

B. & Co. 6133
Made in England

Violino.

Violino.

B. & Cọ 6133

Violino.

B. & Cº 6133. 6773. 13337. 10269

Violino.

Violino.

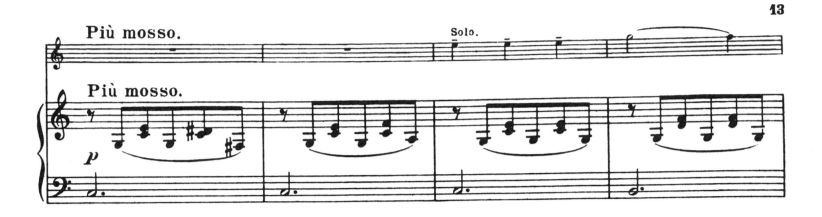

B. & C? 6133. 6773. 13337. 10269

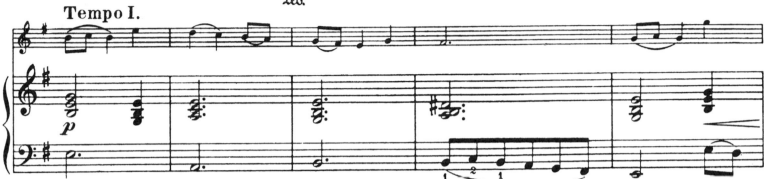

Tempo I.

B. & Cº 6133. 6773. 13337. 10269

Allegro.

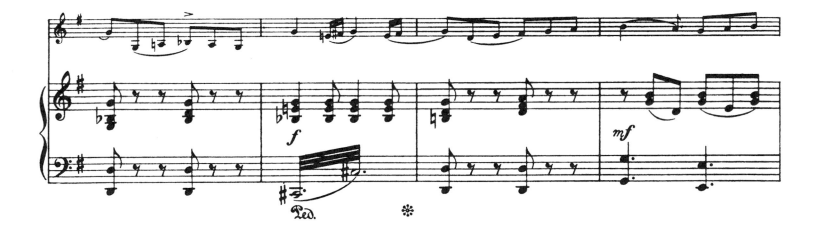

STRING ORCHESTRA
ORCHESTRE A CORDES
STREICHORCHESTER
ORCHESTRA D'ARCHI

The following concertos and concertinos from the list are available with full string orchestral accompaniment:

Nachstehende Konzerte und Concertinos aus unserem Angebot sind mit voller Streichorchester-Begleitung lieferbar:

Les concertos et les concertinos de la liste suivante sont disponibles avec leur accompagnement d'orchestre à cordes:

I seguenti concerti e concertini come da lista sono disponibili con accompagnamento d'orchestra d'archi:

このリストにあるコンチェルトとコンチェルティノスは
すべて完全なストリング・オーケストラの伴奏付きです。

*Kuchler	Opus 12	*Portnoff	Opus 13	Seitz	Opus 15
*Kuchler	Opus 15	Rieding	Opus 34	Seitz	Opus 22
*Millies	(In the style of Mozart)	*Rieding	Opus 35	Ten Have	Opus 30

SELECTED PIECES FROM HANDEL edited by Felix Borowski

AUSGEWÄHLTE STÜCKE VON HÄNDEL herausgegeben von Felix Borowski

PIECES CHOISIES DE HAENDEL éditées par Félix Borowski

SELEZIONI DI PEZZI DI HÄNDEL curate da Felix Borowski

ヘンデル小品集 フェリックス・ボロウスキ 校閲

Bourree   Gavotte   Hornpipe   Largo   Menuet   Musette   Sarabande

*SIX VERY EASY PIECES in the First Position by Edward Elgar

*SECHS SEHR LEICHTE STÜCKE in der Ersten Lage von Edward Elgar

*SIX PIECES TRES FACILES dans la Première Position d'Edward Elgar

*SEI PEZZI MOLTO FACILI in Prima Posizione di Edward Elgar

*やさしい小品6曲集 ファースト・ポジション エドワード・エルガー 校閲

All these are available with Piano, 1st Violin, 2nd Violin, 3rd Elementary Violin, 4th Violin (in lieu of Viola), Viola, 'Cello and Double Bass.
   * Also with additional parts for woodwind, brass and percussion.

Alle angeführten Werke lieferbar mit Klavier, 1. Violine, 2. Violine, 3. Violine (Obligat), 4. Violine (an Stelle von Viola), Viola, 'Cello und Kontrabaß.
   * auch mit zusätzlichen Stimmen für Holzblasinstrumente, Blechbläser und Schlagzeug.

Tous sont disponibles avec piano, 1er violon, 2ème violon, 3ème violon (élémentaire), 4ème violon (à la place de l'alto), alto, violoncelle et contrebasse.
   * Disponibles aussi avec les parties supplémentaires de bois, cuivres et percussions.

Tutti questi pezzi sono disponibili per pianoforte, primo violino, secondo violino, terzo violino semplice, quarto violino (al posto della viola), viola, violoncello e contrabasso.
   * anche con parti aggiuntive per strumenti a fiato, ottoni e strumenti a percussione.

これらはすべて、ピアノ、第1バイオリン、第2バイオリン、
第3エリメンタリー・バイオリン、第4バイオリン、ビオラ、
チェロ、ダブルベースのパート付きです。

   * ウッドウインド、ブラス、パーカッションのパートもあります。

BOSWORTH